A First Book of
MOZART

for the Beginning Pianist

with Downloadable MP3s

Edited by
DAVID DUTKANICZ

DOVER PUBLICATIONS, INC.
Mineola, New York

All songs available as downloadable MP3s!

Go to: http://www.doverpublications.com/0486446247
to access these files.

Dedicated to Anna and Peter

Bibliographical Note

A First Book of Mozart is a new work, first published by Dover Publications,
Inc., in 2005.

International Standard Book Number

ISBN-13: 978-0-486-44624-0
ISBN-10: 0-486-44624-7

Manufactured in the United States by RR Donnelley
44624707   2016
www.doverpublications.com

Contents

Works are arranged in order of approximate difficulty.

Editor's Note

The latest in Dover's renowned series, *My First Book of Mozart* is meant to bring the joys of Mozart's music to beginning pianists. These carefully selected and arranged pieces are designed to develop both the hands and ears, as well as introduce the more memorable masterpieces of the composer. Most of the works focus on a special skill: e.g., double octaves and syncopation in the opening of *Symphony No. 25,* and imitation in the *Minuet in D.* Fingerings are provided as suggestions since each set of hands playing these pieces is different. Teachers and students will be the best judges of that. Also, phrasing and pedaling are left open so as to make the music less daunting for the beginner. These too can be filled in as the student progresses.

Allegro

(K 525)

This is the opening to one of Mozart's most famous works, *Eine Kleine Nachtmusik*, which means "A Little Night Music". It was composed in 1787 while Mozart was living in Vienna. Be sure to keep the music light and flowing.

Allegro

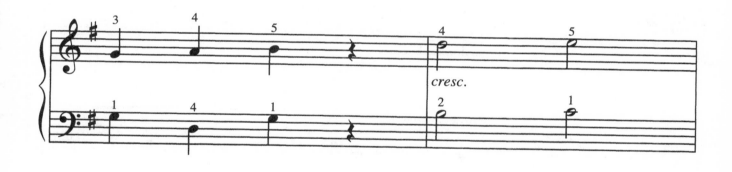

Romanze

(K 525)

Here is the second movement of *Eine Kleine Nachtmusik*. All together there are four movements. Mozart wrote of a fifth, but it was unfortunately lost. The mood here should be a bit calmer, in contrast to the lively first movement.

4

Minuet

A minuet is a slow and stately dance in 3/4 time. This minuet is from one of Mozart's most famous operas, *Don Giovanni*. The characters all dance onstage at the end of Act I to this lovely melody.

Moderato

Papageno's Song

Not all operas are serious and stuffy. Mozart's *Magic Flute* is a fairy-tale opera with a prince, a girl to be rescued, a wizard, and a comical bird catcher dressed in feathers called Papageno. "Yes I am the bird catcher," he sings, "always cheerful, well-known everywhere! If only I could catch a sweet young girl so that she could be all mine!"

Light and Lively

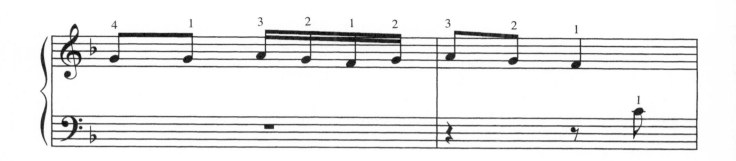

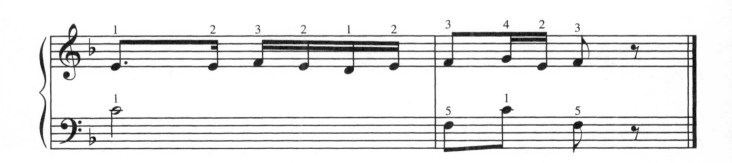

Serenade

A serenade is a song of love. In olden times, it was performed under someone's window at night with a romantic moonlight in the background. This serenade is from the opera *Don Giovanni*, sung by the main character to his love. Try to play it as if you were singing along.

Andante

(K 467)

This is one of Mozart's most popular melodies, taken from *Piano Concerto No. 21*. Ever since it was played in a movie it's gained a nickname, "Elvira Madigan". Play it gracefully, and give the two notes with sharps an extra push.

Romanze

(K 466)

All together, Mozart wrote 27 piano concertos–the first one written in 1767 when he was only 11years old! This famous melody is from the second movement of *Piano Concerto No. 20*. You may even have heard it somewhere before.

Andante

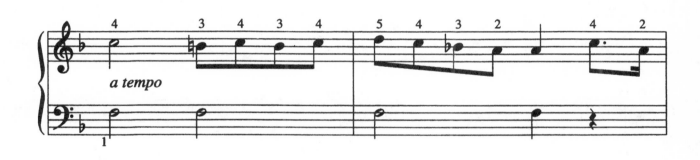

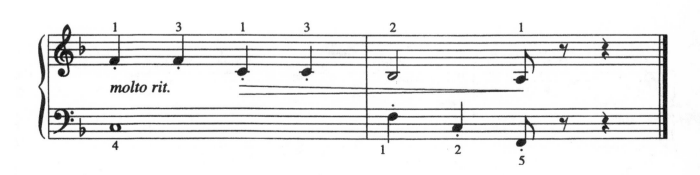

Sleigh Ride

(K 605)

Sleigh Ride is the third of *Three German Dances* which Mozart wrote in 1791. Originally for orchestra, the repeated notes remind us of jingling sleigh bells while the melody in the right hand is like a bumpy ride through the snow.

Trio

(K 605)

Another theme from the *Three German Dances* is this *Trio*. Trios are usually second melodies in a dance. Keep the same light mood as from the *Sleigh Ride*.

Minuet

(K 1)

This charming minuet comes from a collection of small pieces named *Nannerl's Notebook*, after the composer's older sister. Amazingly, those small pieces were composed when he was only six years old and were his first works to be published. Hence, they're cataloged as K 1.

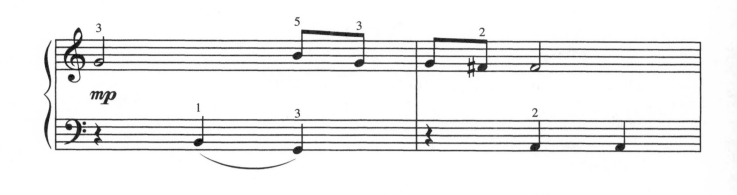

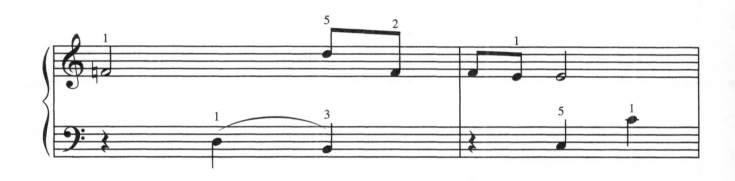

Aria

Here's another piece from the famous opera *Don Giovanni*, this time an aria. Sung by a solo voice, an aria allows a character to express their thoughts and feelings uninterrupted. Feel free to hum or sing along!

Overture

An overture is an introduction to an opera, where the main themes are introduced and the story is outlined–much like a movie trailer. This overture is from *The Marriage of Figaro*, where the story plays like a soap opera. Figaro is set to marry his love Susanna only to have an old count return and try to steal her away. The overture sets the tone for this lively story.

Presto

Twinkle Twinkle Little Star

(K 265)

Here is a popular tune that you'll recognize. The original title is *Ah! Vous Dirai-je Maman*, which means "Oh! I Would Tell You Mom". Follow the notes closely, the original is a little different from what you may be used to. Mozart also wrote 12 variations on this theme. Can you count how many differences there are between the original and the variation on page 20?

Lullaby

(K 350)

This lullaby was originally written for voice and piano. The opening words are: "Never a sound does arise, everyone slumbering lies". Be sure to play gently and follow the dynamics.

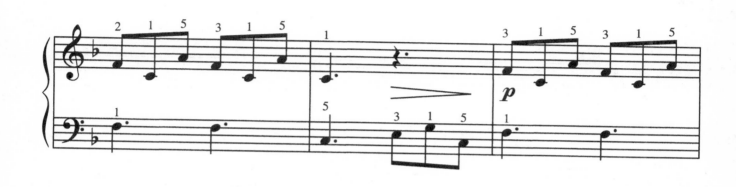

Andante

(K 331)

Mozart wrote 19 sonatas for piano, and this is the opening theme to *Piano Sonata No.11*. The melody is very elegant, which is why he wanted it played *Andante grazioso*, meaning "at a gracefully walking pace".

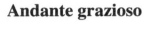

Andante grazioso

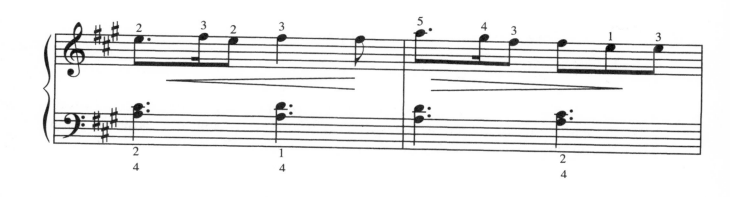

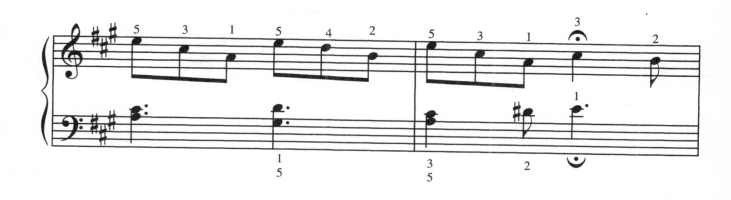

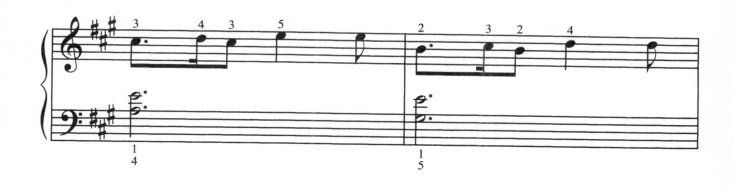

Lento

(K 622)

In Mozart's time, the clarinet was a brand new instrument, not widely known. His concerto was the first of its kind and made the clarinet a popular instrument. And remember, a clarinetist has to breathe. Shape your phrases as if you were breathing to the music.

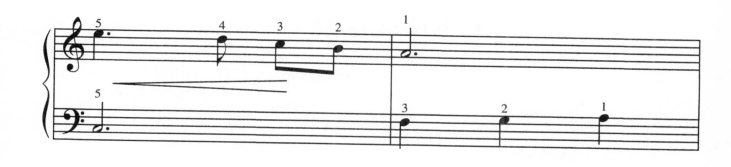

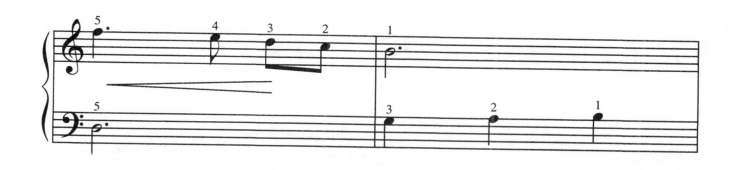

Glockenspiel

This piece is from the opera *Magic Flute*. In this scene, Papageno, the feathered bird catcher, appears on stage and plays magical bells that make grumpy people happy again. Play the notes brightly, as if you were playing bells and making grumpy people happy.

Allegro Moderato

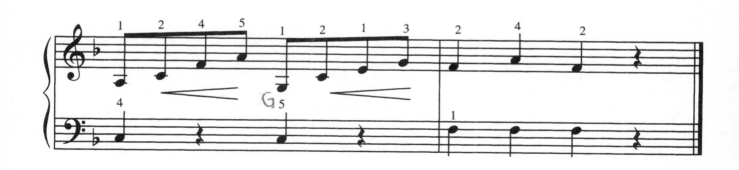

Aria

Here is an aria from *Marriage of Figaro* where one of the characters compares his love to a
butterfly and promises to "never let her fly away again". Listen to how Mozart paints the image
of a butterfly flying and landing by having the melody rise up and then flutter back down.

Tempo di Marcia

Minuet in D

(K 94)

Mozart wrote many minuets. He was so proficient that he created a game where he would write minuets by rolling dice! In this one, the right and left-hand trade phrases. Look for the imitation, and try to create an echo.

Lively, but not too fast

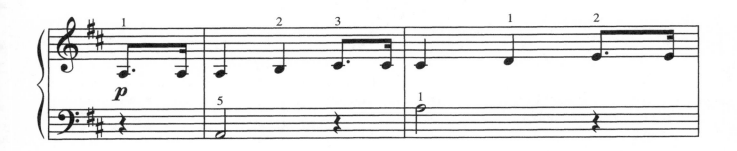

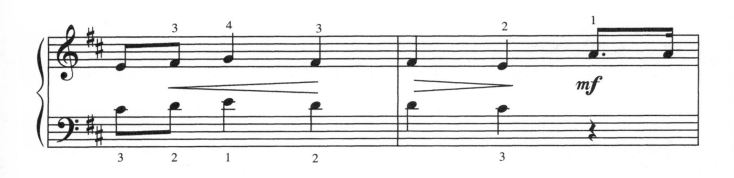

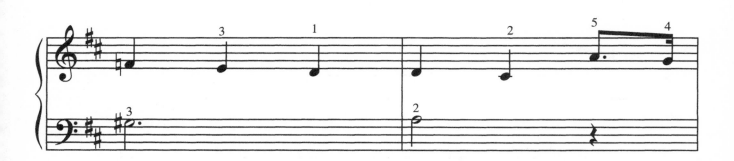

Allegro

(K 417)

This theme is taken from the last movement of Mozart's *Horn Concerto No. 2*. The horn was widely used at hunting events, where it would play special "calls" at the beginning and end of a meet. Play the piece with the same energy and excitement.

Allegro

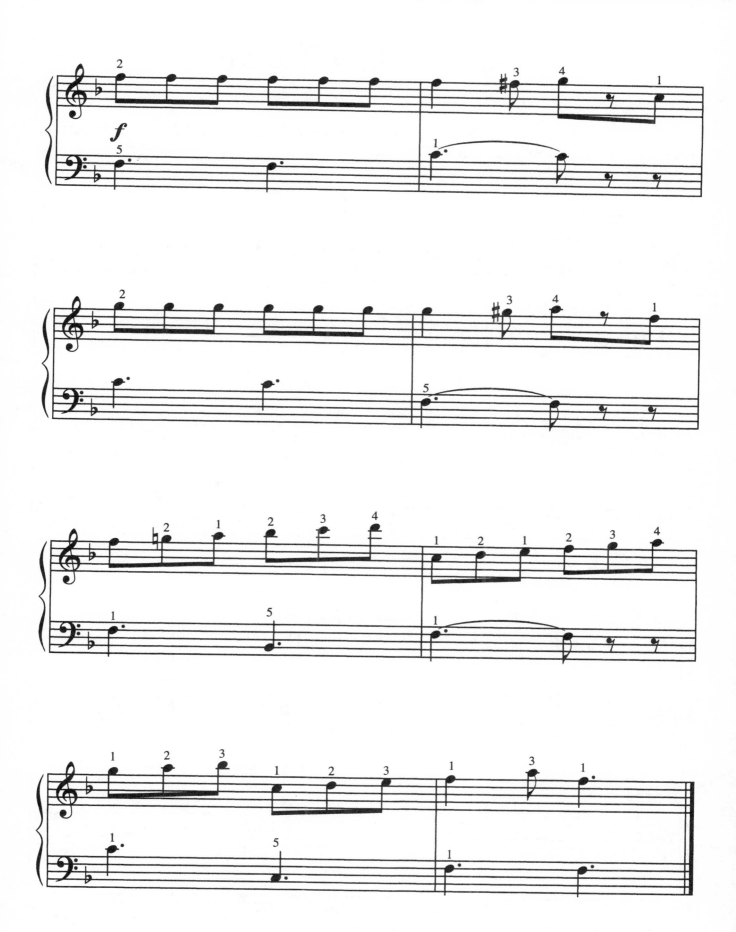

Ronda Alla Turca

(K 331)

This well-known melody is from the third movement of the *Piano Sonata No. 11*–the first movement is on page 24. The notes can be a bit tricky, but be sure to keep a nice and even pace and contrast the *piano* and *forte* sections.

Allegretto

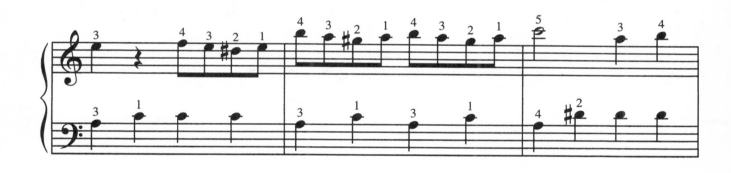

Symphony No. 25

(K 183)

This is the opening to one of Mozart's most famous symphonies. The notes are far apart in the beginning so that the piano can have a nice big sound, almost like a full orchestra. Try to hear the strings playing the crisp syncopation in the beginning.

Allegro con brio

Symphony No. 40

(K 550)

Mozart wrote 41 symphonies in his lifetime, this being his second to last. Amazingly, he wrote over 600 pieces before he tragically died at the young age of 35. We can only imagine how many wonderful symphonies and other pieces he could have written.

Allegro molto

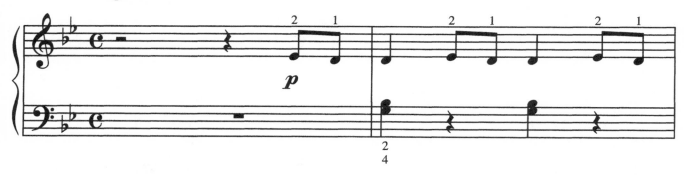

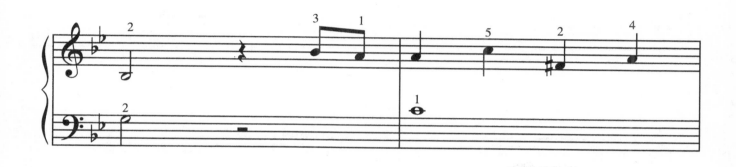

Allegro

(K 310)

The opening theme to Piano Sonata No. 8 is a lively *Allegro maestoso*, meant to be played "quickly and majestically". Like some other selections, this work is in a minor key. Contrast the *piano* and *forte* sections, but also contrast the major and minor.

Allegro maestoso

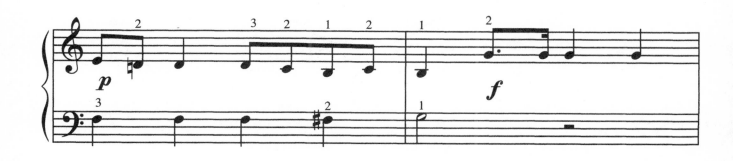

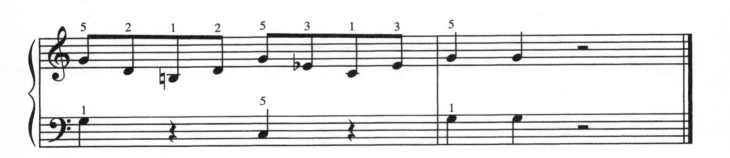